ADJECTIVES
Making Yourself Whole From The Inside Out

Deborah A. Franklin
Deborough's Ministries

Dedication

This book is dedicated to the real women who sowed into me more than they would ever know Great Grandmother Millie (Mama) Goodwin, Grandmother Nita (Mama Nita) Marie Holiday Robinson, Grandmother Mabel (Gram) Franklin and my mother Ola Franklin.

Autonomy

Dedication

Justification

Edification

Confidence

Tenacity

Innovation

Vivacious

Endurance

Sensuous

Adjectives ©2004 Deborah Franklin

Tall, bald, ugly, skinny, fat, stupid, dumb, unattractive,
weird,
Are all words that send your life
Into a frenzy.

You will never marry, your biological
clock is about to stop ticking.

As I shiver at night hearing all the adjective from my past.
You're stupid, you're fat, you're not the one for me.
Good for the one night stand, but never the one to meet
your mother.

Why God?
Why me?
Why do these adjectives fill my space?
Why do I have to be the fat girl, but you have a pretty
face?

Why couldn't I have been the debutant, with the long
flowing hair and the hour glass figure; the one that all the
guys woo and pine after?

Then God reminded me that I was smart, successful,
energetic and full of life.
So deal with your life and look for your new adjectives.

What is an Adjective?
A word that describes a noun.
I am that noun
Caring, funny, successful, radiant, exciting, exuberant,
beautiful, graceful and loving.

AUTONOMY

-the state of existing or acting separately from others.

Philippians 4:8New Revised Standard Version (NRSV)
[8] *Finally, beloved, whatever is true, whatever is honorable, whatever is just, whatever is pure, there is any excellence and if there is anything worthy of praise, think about these things.*

What adjectives are you using to describe yourself? Whether you're a size 4 or 44 remember you are beautiful. You have to start thinking that. How you perceive yourself is key to your success as a woman.

We play so many head games with ourselves and we don't even realize it. If you look closely in your past you can see where this started. I looked as some old pictures of myself as a child. I seemed so happy and full of high self-esteem. I began to wonder, where did this girl go? Where did all of the hope and life in her eyes go?

I started to hear all the adjectives that had been thrown my way over the years. Yes, I was the "chubby" girl in school. I was the "fat" cousin. I remember a cousin telling me one time "Jump off the porch and let me see if the earth rumbles," "Your worldwide," or hearing "your too fat you will never get married or have a boyfriend." Who ever said "Sticks and stones may break my bones, but names will never hurt me," was a liar!
As a young girl this shaped my mind as an adult. So, yes I did make dumb decisions. I never thought I had

any self-worth. So I submersed myself in my work, my education and yes even into church. Yeah....I said it church. These areas never seemed to judge me for my size. This might be why I blossomed to ripe old weight of 365 pounds.

Bottom line, I didn't love me for me. Then one day I looked good and said. "Dam you look good!!!" I said it one time then I said it another time until it started to replace the other negative things I was hearing in my head. I decided to start to work on the weight. I lost 160 pounds with some help form bariatric surgery. Although, I lost the weight I still played head games with myself, because that old chick was still in there. At this moment I began to take autonomy in my life.

We have to have autonomy in our lives as women. On the day to day we take care of so many people, but forget to take care of ourselves. We are the mothers, sisters, teachers, doctors, wives, etc. Whatever role you're in, when do you take time for yourself? Autonomy equates to change. In order to take control of our lives we have to change our perceptions of ourselves. We have to separate our self-perceptions from the perception of others.

When I started to change the way I perceived myself I also notice others started to perceive me differently as well. I began to change my perception with little things. Remember ladies you don't have to spend a lot of money to make a change. Go to Wal-Mart and

buy yourself a new pair of panties, ain't nothing like it. Whether they are cotton or lace you will feel different. Stop wearing raggedy under garments!

AUTONOMY!!! I'm sure you are saying what do new underwear have to do with autonomy. Well, let me tell you. What you wear underneath is a reflection of how you feel on the inside (most of which came from the perceptions of others); so when you wear raggedy underwear you're saying to yourself "Raggedy is who I am underneath (inside).

Ladies, we have to start to think on things that are true. You were put here on this earth for a purpose. You have to know that you are excellent in every way. You were created to be different. Start to look at yourself as an asset and not a liability. You do have worth and can't nobody take it from you, but you have to know it. I know that you're thinking we were taught not to be arrogance....guess what seeing our own self-worth. Think about it like this: a Hershey candy bar and a Godiva candy bar, are both chocolate, but when you go to purchase you expect to pay more for Godiva. Why? Because of the value that is put on it. So are you a Hershey or Godiva?

Now, let's take a closer look at our self-perception. When you refer to yourself it has to be in the positive. Ok, you may have a few extra pounds, don't say you're fat. I like the term "fluffy" or my favorite "Voluptuous." Let's work through this sheet together to start to change the perception of ourselves. Now remember if it's something that can be changed, such as losing weight. Start with easy obtainable goals, like just 5 pounds instead of 40. Now let's get started on changing ourselves.

Self-Image

1. Identify three areas in your life you would like to change.

_____

_____

_____

2. What prevents you from changing the above noted items?

_____

_____

_____

_____

3. What negative adjectives has someone placed on you?

_____

_____

_____

_____

4. What steps are you taking to change them?

_____

_____

_____

_____

5. What negative adjectives have you placed on yourself?

_____

_____

_____

_____

_____

6. What steps are you taking to reverse them?

_____

_____

_____

_____

Autonomy 4 Week Plan

Week	Goal	Accomplished
1		
2		
3		
4		

Prayer

Lord give me the strength to gain autonomy over my life. Let me take control of my actions and thoughts. Let me change my perception of myself. I know that if I get control of me then I can get to know you better as well. Increase my faith in myself. I cast down to the pits of hell all of the voices of my past decisions, actions, relationships, jobs and most of all the "I can't do it, I'm not good enough" right to the pits of hell. God I declare and decree that Autonomy will be present in my life. I am independent and I am free in my will and my actions. Amen.

Notes

Dedication
    -the quality of being dedicate or committed to a task or purpose.

Romans 12:2 (NRSV)
Do not be conformed to this world,[a] but be transformed by the renewing of your minds, so that you may discern what is the will of God—what is good and acceptable and perfect.

Are you dedicated or obligated? Yes, there is a difference. Ok, let me talk to what I know and some of you can relate to this as well. I grew up in the church and knew all the church lingo. I could tell what was going to happen before it happened. I was in the mix. Every time the church door opened, I was there. Hmmmm did you hear me say at any time I was there for the Word or who got saved? Nope, I was there out of obligation. I wasn't dedicated to God, and truth be told...nothing else either. I was just going through the motions.

Now, when the light bulb came on. I started to realize that I was not doing any good to myself or others and then I began to think about Esther. Yes, I did pay attention in Sunday School, I just wasn't applying what I was learning. My mind needed to be renewed.

Esther was dedicated to herself. She never let her surroundings intimidate her, she stayed committed to her course. Although all of the other women were basking in the sunshine and taking advantage of the Kings court, she stayed true to herself. She never tried to take advantage of the situation.

Now, I'm not going to tell you that Esther didn't like nice things or having the best of everything, but she didn't let it take her out of her character. Yes, she liked designer handbags and shoes, but I just have to believe that she was an observer.

She was a watcher of her surroundings. She looked at how the other women were carrying themselves and she just didn't want to be that woman. She knew she had to be different to catch the eye of the king.

Esther was also dedicated to not putting her business in the street. She never told anyone that she was Jewish and her family situation. She was just herself. She was confident in who she was. She didn't let the world transform her.

So many times we get caught up in our pedigree and get lost in tradition and never truly get to know who we are. We are someone's mother, sister, teacher, coworker, cousin, etc. We get caught up in everyone else's identity and we are more dedicated to it than they are. You know their ins, outs and schedule better than they know it themselves.

The sad part is-someone were to ask you "What your favorite color? "; "What's your favorite place to travel?" and "Why?"; you may not be able to answer. However, if those same questions were asked of your about the one you are dedicated to; you could answer every question with great detail. Now to add insult to injury the one you are dedicated to is not yourself....Now that did make you think?

Today is the day you rededicate to you.

Prayer

Lord, today grant me the ability to dedicate myself to myself. I want to be whole and be all that I know that I can be. In dedicating myself to find the true me, not to be influenced by society or others but to be like Esther, true to myself.

My favorite color is

_____

My favorite place to travel is

_____

My favorite food is

_____

This makes me happy

_____

_____

_____

	Why	Steps to Change	Outcome
Area I			
Area II			
Area III			

Notes

Justification

-the action of showing something to be right or reasonable.

Theology-The action of declaring or making righteous in the sight of God.

Ephesians 2:1-10

2 And you were dead in the trespasses and sins 2 in which you once walked, following the course of this world, following the prince of the power of the air, the spirit that is now at work in the sons of disobedience— 3 among whom we all once lived in the passions of our flesh, carrying out the desires of the body[a] and the mind, and were by nature children of wrath, like the rest of mankind.[b] 4 But[c] God, being rich in mercy, because of the great love with which he loved us, 5 even when we were dead in our trespasses, made us alive together with Christ—by grace you have been saved— 6 and raised us up with him and seated us with him in the heavenly places in Christ Jesus,7 so that in the coming ages he might show the immeasurable riches of his grace in kindness toward us in Christ Jesus. 8 For by grace you have been saved through faith. And this is not your own doing; it is the gift of God, 9 not a result of works, so that no one may boast. 10 For we are his workmanship, created in Christ Jesus for good works, which God prepared beforehand, that we should walk in them.

I can't because I had a child out of wedlock; I can't because I didn't graduate from the right school; I can't because I'm single; I can't because I'm married; I can't because I was once labeled as a whore; I can't because, because, because and because. So many times in life we let the judgment of others shape the judgment of ourselves. We walk around playing head games with ourselves and we never reach our fullest potential since we have a bad case of the "I Can'ts" Yes, I do know I just made up a word, but you know what I mean.

Today is the day you enter a zone where your past sins and mistakes are justified. This may seem strange, but guess what you're still here to tell the story. So many times we lose our present by our past: but if that past didn't happen, then our present and future wouldn't be what it is. According to Ephesians 2:1-10 As we have evolved and we have relinquished worldly things, we have to be able to move on from there.

I have met so many people who stand in judgment of others, but never look at themselves. They can see the wrong in everyone else, but fail to look at what they are doing. They are quick to say, "I'm not committing the top 5 sins" but my reply to that is sin is sin. Deliverance or change can't happen until we look at the whole picture of ourselves. We just can't look at the part that people see, but we have to deal with our secret selves.

The secret self the one behind closed doors who plots against others in their mind or who has under cover road rage. When you are judging someone else, you think or say things like: "I'm not like her," "I don't do that," but if you look a little closer you're doing something. Whatever that something is you are making it right in your own mind---justifying it. Instead we have to look at our secret selves from God's perspective and determine whether or not we are justified from His point of view.

Prayer

God forgive me of all my sins and transgressions that I have committed by thoughts words or deeds. I know that I have not been right in all of my decisions, but I do have justification. I thank you for past mistakes because they have made me who I am. I forgive myself for holding on to the past and not letting myself move forward. I forgive myself for letting my past hold me in bondage. I forgive myself for doubting that I am better than who others say or think that I am. God I thank you for your revelation and give me peace as I move forward.

What three areas do you have Justification in that you need to release to move forward.

	Steps to Change	Outcome
Area I		
Area II		
Area III		

Notes

Edification
-the instruction or improvement of a person morally or intellectually

2 Timothy 2:15 King James Version(KJV)

[15] Study to shew thyself approved unto God, a workman that needeth not to be ashamed, rightly dividing the word of truth.

You may be thinking right now she was doing good up to this point, but now she wants me to be selfish. Guess what.....You are right!!!!!

We constantly worry about others so much that we forget about ourselves. What have you done to teach yourself today? What have you done to change something about yourself today?

Now let's take it a little deeper what have you learned from your past? I know it can be dark, but trust me there is some light. I get it; you're asking, what can be learned from the rape, mistrust, not feeling loved, feeling alone, feeling used and abused; yeah I really do get it. But there is a lesson if nothing else you're stronger then what you thought and most of all you're a survivor. Which leads to the edification of others.

At one point I would sit back and wonder why me God? Why did I have to experience being taken advantage of, why did I have to have the miscarriage, why did I have to be lied to, or never achieving the so called American Dream?

God had to remind me that I am not in control. He is. In other words I had to go where he was taking me and I had to have all those experiences to become who He wanted me to be. I had to stop putting my time table on it and wait for His direction.

How can you say God is a healer and you've never been healed from anything? How can you say God is a deliverer and you have never been delivered from anything? How can you say God is a comforter and you've never been comforted? You see everything we go through is for edification. After having those experiences you can now edify others.

What is your testimony?

_____

_____

_____

_____

_____

_____

_____

_____

_____

_____

_____

_____

_____

_____

Prayer

God today grant me the peace that I need to learn from my past. Let me be able to provide edification not only to others, but to myself. I want to be used at this time and not live in the shame of my past. I will not feel guilty for taking time for myself to improve myself and to expand who I am. Thank you God for all you've done and I commit to the edification of myself and others.

Notes

Confidence
-the feeling of belief that one can rely on someone or something; firm trust
-the state of feeling certain about the truth of something
-a feeling of self-assurance arising from one's appreciation of one's own abilities or qualities

Confidence is what we need to survive. Yeah, I know it's hard, but we have to have it. We lose it because of all the head games we play with ourselves. We think I don't have a degree; I didn't come from the right pedigree, etc. I say to that who cares!!!

I can remember growing up my parents worked hard to have us attend some the best schools and live in a good neighborhood. My father was a cross country truck driver and my mother was a homemaker. I went to school with people whose parents were doctors, lawyers, business executives, etc. So you can see how that could be intimidating. But then one day the light bulb went on. If my daddy didn't do his job their fathers couldn't do theirs.

So think about this, without you someone won't or rather can't make it to their next level. Your mind set or your skill set is what they need. What if Esther didn't have the confidence in herself to go and speak to the king, her family would have been lost.

Take this time to take a self inventory of your gifts and talents. Figure out what is your God given talent and start to develop it more. Many of you may be amazed at the outcome. It's ok to take some test to see where your strengths and weakness are.

Prayer

God today grant me the confidence to exceed my own expectations. Allow me to work in excellence and gain the favor with those I need to propel myself to the next level. God for all the fights I've had to fight grant me a sweat less victory in the areas I'm believing to build my confidence in.

Check out these websites and record your findings.
Most of all try to implement your findings.

http://www.humanmetrics.com/cgi-win/jtypes2.asp

Findings

_____

_____

_____

http://www.16personalities.com/free-personality-test

Findings

_____

_____

_____

http://www.spiritualgiftstest.com/test/adult

Findings

_____

_____

_____

Notes

Tenacity
        -the quality or fact of being able to grip something firmly; grip

Luke 17:32 (NIV)

32 Remember Lot's wife!

What are you holding on to and won't let go? Look at it from both sides of the coin. Stop it!!! Don't be deep here, truly be honest with yourself. Look at your life from the spiritual and the practical. Are you holding on to a ministry that you need to move from? Are you holding on to a relationship that you need to let go? Remember Lot's wife!

Lot was told to leave Sodom and Gomorra with his family and don't look back. I would just have to imagine his wife was thinking, you're asking me to leave all of what I know. Go somewhere and I don't know anyone. Forget about all the good times that I had. Seriously, you're telling me to leave my house, my car, my job, my family, etc. You can't be serious," but God was serious in his instructions. All she had to do is leave and not look back. She couldn't and turned into a pillar of salt.

Her husband told her to leave a place and not look back. She didn't follow instructions and had to suffer the consequences. What was in the city that she was going to miss that was tugging on her and she couldn't move forward? I don't know but bottom line you don't want get stuck in a place so deep that you end up in quick sand.

For me it was obtaining my degrees for others it may be the path that they have laid out for themselves. In looking over what you're holding on to, is it holding you back from living **your** life to the fullest.

What in your life are your gripping? What do you need to do to endure? Have you sat down and evaluated where you are? There are countless situation where we have to learn when to let go. We hold on for dear life and life is passing us by. I'm guilty of this, I'm the one who has to see it to the end. The true captain of the ship, if it sinks I'm going down with it. In retrospect, maybe that's why it has taken me so long to reach some of the goals I had, because I didn't know when to let go.

Tenacity can be a gift and a curse. We often hold tight to people, relationships, jobs, etc., when we need to be more tenacious in developing ourselves to reach a higher level.

What do you need to let go in order to move forward?

_____

_____

_____

_____

_____

_____

_____

_____

_____

_____

_____

_____

_____

_____

_____

Prayer

God today grant me the courage to evaluate what I'm holding on to that I need to let go. Give me the power and strength that I need to move on and not look back. I don't want to be like Lots wife and turn in to a pillar of salt because I couldn't move on to the next level in my destiny. God let me have tenacity in depending on you in all that I do. Give me tenacity in developing who I am and to be a better servant to you. God I know this is my season and my time to be who you have called me to be, but I know I can't get there if I keep holding on to what I need to let go of. God do it now. Amen.

Notes

Innovation

- the process of translating an idea or invention into a good or service that creates value or for which customers will pay.

Proverbs 31:17-18 (NIV)
[17] She sets about her work vigorously;
   her arms are strong for her tasks.
[18] She sees that her trading is profitable,
   and her lamp does not go out at night.

Are you sick and tired of being sick and tired? Why are you settling for what is not who you really are. Why are you staying in this seat of complacency? God has not put you here to just be ok with getting by and being mundane.

Get up and do something about it. It's time for you to take control of yourself and take it to the next level of who you are destined to be. Destiny, can be gained when we don't settle for what is in front of us. We have to seek after the "impossible dream". Do you think we would have ever made it to the moon if we continued to listen to the folk who said it was impossible?

I know if you have grown up in church or ever been to a Women's Day event. You have heard the story of the virtuous woman. But, there is something more there than a cliché'. Look closer, she works vigorously and her trading is profitable. Meaning she not only had a skill, but she knows how to make a profit from it. She takes something and gives it value and finds success.

Ok your money is funny virtuous woman. What are you doing about it? Do you have a skill that has value to others?

Of course you do. For example, you may have a gift of cleaning. You can't stand to see things dusty or in disarray. More importantly you are an excellent cleaner and organizer. Share the gift; look for people who are not gifted in that area. Offer your cleaning and organizing services for a fee.

Prayer

God today grant me the boldness to activate my innovative idea. I know that this is my season to make it happen. Give me the courage to stand in the midst of trial and tribulation that may be around me. God give me the wisdom to trust myself and do what I know that has to be done to make an impact on community and the nation. God, I know that I am appointed and called to this area of my life.

What three innovative ideas do you have that you know you can turn in to another stream of income?

Do research on that area to see what the going rate is nationally and locally.

Recognize your worth.

Make your business cards.

Most of all get busy.

Notes

Vivacious
   - happy and lively in a way that is attractive

Ezekiel 36:26 (NIV)
[26] I will give you a new heart and put a new spirit in you; I will remove from you your heart of stone and give you a heart of flesh.

Now is the time for you to leave the masquerade party. Yes, I said it. You're sitting around with a mask on hiding who you really are. Cosmetics can only do so much for you. You're all dressed up and made up on the outside, and falling apart on the inside.

As women we are always taught to hide our feelings and be who we are supposed to be at this appointed time. We truly have to seek out a new heart, because we want our spirit renewed. We can't be successful or happy if we are holding on and our hearts have turned to stone.

We never really have learned to show who we really are. Do you remember being told "Good girls don't ask those type of questions", "Good girls don't go to those type of places," or "Good girls don't hang around those type of people." Yes, that may have been correct, but as a leader we need to be exposed to many different aspects of life. No, I'm not saying you need to be at the extreme, but live a little. Even Jesus was in the midst of sinners. How can you be a light if you have never been in the dark?

Now, the biggest mask of all....take it off the Mask of Shame. A lot of us live in shame because we don't want anyone to know the details of our deliverance;

the specific sins we committed. We don't want to hear this infamous phrase "No not her, I thought she was a good girl" I'm sick of it! We are deeply concerned about the opinions of women that we can't get delivered or accept the deliverance we have already received.

I will share one of my darkest secrets. One that sent me into a depression that I thought I would not come out of. In August of 2011 I had a miscarriage. I know you're thinking it's nothing wrong with that but the circumstances that surrounded it were a bit of a mess. I was single and just getting started in ministry. I'm pregnant? I really wanted a child, but not like this. Now to make matters worse, this pregnancy was a result of date rape. Those closest to me at the time had no idea that I was pregnant or had a miscarriage. Why? Because I wore the Mask of Shame.

I found out I was pregnant on a Monday and had a miscarriage on Friday. This was the start of my spiraling out of control once the reality, hurt and shame kicked in. I cried every day so after this traumatic event, I would come to church and cry during all the services. I couldn't stand to be around other with babies or small children. Yes indeed I was in a bad place.

I felt all alone and the truth of the matter I was. I didn't really have anyone I could talk to that would not judge me, but I tried to talk to someone who I thought I could trust and they said "Sin is sin" In my mind I'm thinking really....I just lost my child. I'm thinking how you can say something so hurtful. I spiraled to a place of almost no return.

Then I was able to talk to a friend who didn't judge me. Who had just gone through this same situation with her daughter, but I didn't know it until I shared my story. I had just found my place of solace. I was able to really cry and talk it out in a safe place. She prayed for me and gave me encouraging words. Now I know that I can empathize with someone who is going through the loss of a child. I can stand with them and be able to say. God is truly in control and will give you peace.

You may not have gone through something so horrific, but what mask are you wearing that is holding you back. Which mask is hiding your biggest testimony, the one that can help others heal? I know this is a cliché, but our trials and tribulations only come to make us strong. We can't have a testimony unless we have a test. Fortunately, we don't have to do it alone. Tell your story it will break that Mask of Shame and it will help heal others. So many times we walk in the world alone and we don't have to. It's simple: give your testimony and demolish the shame and Be yourself.

You will be amazed that once the shame is gone how happy and truly VIVACIOUS you will really be.

Prayer

God today grant me the courage to take the mask off. I know I can't truly be whole until I'm healed from what I'm hiding. Let my past be my past and let my testimony be healing for me and for others who hear it. God, let me be a woman of wisdom and who is not ashamed of where I've come from and who I am. Let me accept the real me and not the-me that has hidden behind the mask. Amen.

What mask are your wearing that you need to remove, to become VIVACIOUS!

Notes

Endurance

- the ability to do something difficult for a long time

-the ability to deal with pain or suffering that continues for a long time

- the quality of continuing for a long time

Ecclesiastes 9:11 (NIV)
[11] I have seen something else under the sun:
The race is not to the swift
    or the battle to the strong,
nor does food come to the wise
    or wealth to the brilliant
    or favor to the learned;
but time and chance happen to them all.

The race is not given to the swift, but to the one who endures to the end. We don't want to wait for anything. We want it now! We don't want it to continue, because we don't want the pain or the struggle to make it to the end. We think in life it should always be easy.

If you were to ask an athlete they would say no pain no gain. You have to put tension on the muscle in order for it to get stronger. This is just like our faith. There has to be some tension to make it grow stronger. My parents would say you will never really appreciate anything if you never work for it.

I would be inclined to believe this is why we have generations of people now who feel they are entitled to everything. They feel as though it should be given to them. They want it now. No responsibility, no consequences for their actions. They think they should be able to do what they want and not respect their elders.

If we look at Job, he endured so much. No, I'm not saying we have to lose everything that we have, but we must learn how to endure. The hardest part of endurance is not what we are going through, but like Job it's the people around us.

We know what God has told us. We know what our promise is and instead of following His plan. We move too fast, listening to the wrong counsel.

In our time of enduring we also have to evaluate what needs to stay and what needs to let go. We want to hold on to everything. Kenny Rogers may have said it best "You have to know when to hold 'um and know when to fold 'um" Yes, it was talking about playing cards, but it has some practical application as well. As women we tend to have endurance in areas we need to discontinue immediately.

We have endurance on a dead end job, an abusive relationship, a dying ministry, but I like to call this fear. We have a fear of the unknown. We know there is better, however we don't want to branch out and try something different that will make us better. We hide behind "I have to stick it out," or "I got my pension." In all actuality, we are miserable, heartbroken and depression is settling in on the inside.

Not knowing when to let go can lead you down some dark areas that will affect your health and your personality. Your stress level may increase causing your immune system functioning to decrease, cortisone to increase along with your weight and other stress related issues. You will stop being your normally cheerful and easy going self. You will begin to be more cynical and extremely critical of everything and everyone around you. Persevere through the test, just be sure to let it go when it is over. Endure to your impossible dreams.

Prayer

God today grant me endurance I need to fulfill all of the dreams that I have. God, give me the boldness to be like Job and truly trust the faith that I have in, you. I have a spirit of expectation right now that every word and promise that has been spoken into my life that it will come forth. I'm believing that it will come forth and it will manifest right now in the name of Jesus.

Write a good by letter to what has been holding you back, and then burn it.

Notes

Sensuous
> - relating to or affecting the senses rather than the intellect.
> - attractive or gratifying physically, especially sexually

Song of Songs 6:10
Who is this that appears like the dawn,
    fair as the moon, bright as the sun,
    majestic as the stars in procession?

Senses ©2004 Deborah Franklin

You make my senses come alive with passion.

My sense of smell is awakened by your sweet aroma
that emulates from your skin.

Which unlocks my sense of sight that clicks in on the
intense gaze of your eyes.

Makes my knees grow weak and buckle in
anticipation and listening for your next move.

Arouses my sense of hearing. That hears the
steadiness of your voice as you whisper in my ear.

I want to explode when I hear
Your voice that brings forth a shiver of expectation.

My sense of touch is resuscitated while you nibble on
my ear and I feel the soft subtle lips that kiss me ever
so gently on my soft hollowed walls.

A cosmic explosion occurs when all my senses
register their reports that all equal up to you my
tantalizer of my senses.

Whew!!! I know right, yes, I went there. God wants us to get to know this part of our being. Come on Solomon. If you read the Song of Solomon it is the most sensuous book in the bible. Therefore, we must need this in our lives and need to grab hold to it ladies.

This area in our lives looks at our sensual being and not our intellect. We have to take control of what we are really feeling. Take inventory of what we are thinking. What adjectives are we using to describe this area of our lives. For Christian women this area is taboo; we are told not to deal with this area and when we do we look at it as shameful. We should not feel shame in this area, but develop it for our strength.

We may be losing in the area of our families because we don't have a hold on our feelings. We are not honest with ourselves about the way a massage makes us feel. How being touched in the right spot makes us have a tingle. No, it's not a sin. It's natural. Come on now ladies. How can we minister to someone when we are not honest with ourselves about how we truly feel about our own sensuality?

I have seen numerous relationships fail because we were not honest with how we felt or how someone was making us feel. Our senses frequently speak to us way before our intellect does. Have you ever met someone and instantly you knew something was off about them? Had that feeling that I shouldn't go down that street? Yes, your senses or as the saints of ole would say, the "Holy Spirit" was in control.

This is where prayer and fasting comes in. If we sought the face of God and tapped more into the Holy Spirit we may not have to deal with certain areas for a long period of time. Again, leaning more on the spirit of God and not the intellect of God. Listen to your senses, be honest about your sensuality and follow the Spirit.

What makes you feel sensuous?

_____

_____

_____

_____

Once you determine what makes you feel sensuous,
do this for three days. At the end record how you feel
about yourself and the reaction of others.

Self_____

_____

_____

_____

Others_____

_____

_____

_____

Prayer

God today grant me the courage to find who I really am. I know that I am a sensuous being and I want to develop that part of my life more. I want to hear your voice and know that it is you. I want to be able to set a fast and be able to stick to it. I accept that just like Jesus I will be tempted but I most hold on to the word and use it in my defense. God you are who I want to be like more. Holy Spirit, I need you now to give me peace and the ability to tap into a higher level of discernment and freedom to be who you have called me to be in You.

Notes

Contact Information

Website
   www.deboroughs.com

Facebook
   www.facebook.com/deboroughsministries

Twitter
   @mindfranklin

All scriptures came from the New International Version Bible unless otherwise noted. All definition came from Webster Dictionary.

Photography and Graphics by
DSD Photography
donnasflames@yahoo.com